Mary M

Fights for Justice

Kate Broad

Boston, Massachusetts
Chandler, Arizona
Glenview, Illinois
Upper Saddle River, New Jersey

Illustrations
3, 4, 5, 7, 8, 9, 10 Bob Dacey.

Photographs
Every effort has been made to secure permission and provide appropriate credit for photographic material. The publisher deeply regrets any omission and pledges to correct errors called to its attention in subsequent editions.

Unless otherwise acknowledged, all photographs are the property of Pearson Education, Inc.

Photo locators denoted as follows: Top (T), Center (C), Bottom (B), Left (L), Right (R), Background (Bkgd)

Opener: Library of Congress; 1 Library of Congress; 2 Library of Congress; 6 Library of Congress; 12 Library of Congress; 13 Library of Congress; 14 ©Andersen Ross/Blend Images/Getty Images; 15 Library of Congress.

Copyright © 2013 by Pearson Education, Inc., or its affiliates. All rights reserved. Printed in the United States of America. This publication is protected by copyright, and permission should be obtained from the publisher prior to any prohibited reproduction, storage in a retrieval system, or transmission in any form by any means, electronic, mechanical, photocopying, recording, or likewise. For information regarding permissions, write to Pearson Curriculum Rights & Permissions, One Lake Street, Upper Saddle River, New Jersey 07458.

ISBN-13: 978-0-328-67641-5
ISBN-10:   0-328-67641-1

Pearson® is a trademark, in the U.S. and/or in other countries, of Pearson Inc. or its affiliates.

2 3 4 5 6 7 8 9 10 V0FL 15 14 13 12

Unfair Treatment

Mary McLeod Bethune was the fifteenth child in her family. She was the first one born free. The Civil War had ended slavery. Yet, in many ways, African Americans were not really free. They lived under **segregation**. They could not go to the same schools as white Americans or eat in the same restaurants. They could not even use the same water fountains.

Mary McLeod Bethune

Mary McLeod Bethune grew up under segregation. She saw that African American children did not have the same chances in life as white children. She worked her whole life to help African Americans gain **equality**.

The Birth of a Leader

Mary McLeod Bethune was born in South Carolina on July 10th, 1875. Her parents were Patsy and Samuel McLeod. They were once enslaved. Now the family was free and had a farm. Everyone worked hard in the fields. Mary McLeod picked cotton. When she was nine, she could pick 250 pounds of cotton in one day!

You Can't Read That!

It had been against the law to teach slaves to read. So no one in the McLeod family knew how to read. Mary McLeod had never been to school.

Patsy McLeod worked for a white woman. Sometimes Mary McLeod went with her and played with the woman's children. One day, she picked up a book. One of the children told her, "You can't read that—put that down!"

The school Mary McLeod attended may have looked like this one.

A Chance to Learn

Mary McLeod's pride was hurt. She made up her mind. She would learn to read. One day she got her chance. A teacher came to her town to start a school for black children.

She had to walk five miles to and from school each day. Mary McLeod did it gladly. She studied hard and learned quickly.

Becoming a Teacher

Soon she was using her skills to help others. She read letters to her neighbors. She read the Bible to her family. She even taught her brother to read.

When Mary McLeod grew up, she went to South Carolina to teach. There she met a young man named Albertus Bethune. The two got married. Now she was Mary McLeod Bethune.

Building a New School

Bethune wanted to do more. She wanted to build a new school where there weren't any schools for African Americans. She moved to Florida. Many African Americans had moved there.

In 1904, Bethune started a school in Daytona Beach. She called it the Daytona Educational and Industrial Training School for Negro Girls.

Today Bethune's school is a college with more than three thousand students.

At first it was hard to keep the school open. Bethune had no money. She couldn't buy paper or pens for her students. But she was determined. The girls used boxes for seats. They wrote with sticks and ink made from elderberries. Bethune asked people in the community for help. She got it, and the school grew. In two years it had 250 students.

Working for Justice

Bethune worked for justice outside the school, too. In some places there were unfair laws. Some of these laws said people had to pay a tax to vote. Many blacks and poor whites could not afford to pay this **poll tax**. Bethune raised money so African Americans could vote. She also worked to change the law so that women could vote, too.

People began to notice Bethune's work. She became known as an important **civil rights** leader. She was active in many organizations. Through her work with women's groups, Bethune met Eleanor Roosevelt. Her husband, Franklin Delano Roosevelt, was an important government leader. The two women became good friends. They worked on many projects together to help children and African Americans.

Advisor to Presidents

Bethune's school grew into a college. Bethune's reputation grew, too. People in Washington, D.C., noticed Bethune's work. She was even asked to be an **advisor** to Presidents Calvin Coolidge and Herbert Hoover. As an advisor, she gave advice on issues concerning African Americans.

1875 Mary McLeod is born.

1898 Mary McLeod marries Albertus Bethune.

1884 Mary McLeod starts school.

1899 Bethune moves to Florida.

1904 Bethune opens a school in Daytona.

In 1933, Franklin Delano Roosevelt became president. He asked Bethune to be part of an unofficial group of black leaders called the "black cabinet." They gave the president advice. He also named Bethune the director of a federal organization to help African American youth. She was the first black woman to be in charge of a **federal agency**.

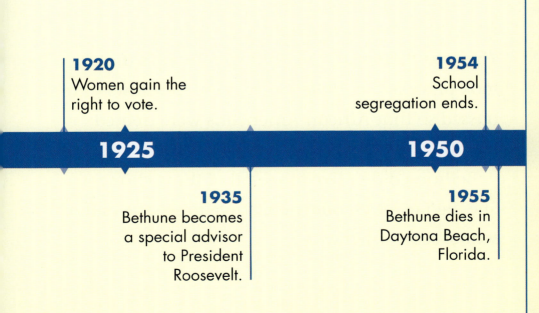

A Change for America

In 1954, the United States Supreme Court made an important decision. The Court said it was against the law to have separate schools for African American students and white students. This was the beginning of many changes that took place in the 1950s and 1960s. New laws were passed so that African Americans were treated equally.

Bethune didn't live to see all of these changes. She died in 1955. But she did live to see the end of school segregation.

Remembering Bethune

Bethune once wrote, "Our aim must be to create a world . . . where no man's skin, color, or religion, is held against him."

Bethune fought her whole life for this goal. Because of her life's work, thousands of African Americans gained greater opportunities.

Glossary

advisor a person who gives advice, suggestions, and ideas to another person

civil rights the rights of a citizen, such as equal treatment under the law

equality having the same rights

federal agency a division of the national government

poll tax money people paid in order to vote

segregation customs and laws that kept people of one race separate from those of another